Take Home the Sea
A Volume of Seaside Poetry

Carol LaForet

DAYS OF YORE PUBLISHING

www.daysofyore.org
P.O. Box 166
Fountainville, PA 18923

Take Home the Sea
A Volume of Seaside Poetry

Days of Yore Publishing
P.O. Box 166
Fountainville, PA 18923 U.S.A.
books@daysofyore.org
www.daysofyore.org

DAYS OF YORE
PUBLISHING

This edition is published by Days of Yore and distributed by www.flutesonline.com.

Publisher's Cataloging-in-Publication
(Provided by Quality Books, Inc.)

LaForet, Carol.
    Take home the sea : a volume of seaside poetry /
Carol LaForet, author. -- 1st ed.
    p. cm.
    LCCN 00-192916
    ISBN 0-9706052-0-X

    1. Sea poetry, American.   I. Title.

PS3562.A3115T35 2000   811'.6
                       QBI00-901956

Take Home the Sea

Contents

Foreword

Some of us crave the sea; we yearn for its broad vistas, its salty mists, the rolling, joyous rise of its swells - and we plot to spend our spare days seaside.

This volume of poetry is written for fellow sea-lovers who, at vacation's end, would surely take the sea home with them if only they could.

It is my hope that when they read these poems they will almost feel sea breezes stirring their hair. . . will practically hear gulls' cries and crashing surf at dawn. . . that through these poems they will indeed be able to **Take Home the Sea.**

C. W. LaForet
Bucks County, PA

This book is dedicated to Walt,
with love and gratitude.

Summer Scroll

The beach is a summer scroll
written with tears of the sea,
surging water
cradled in sandy crators
'til the ocean,
childlike,
reclaims it.

Last summer wilted
on a September morning,
with a promise to return.
Now we are left
with footprints in the sand,
and a sea that wonders
where the children have gone.

Poseidon's Treasure

There is icing on the
ocean tonight;
golden light shimmers
on crests of waves.

Slices of Neptune cake
topple to the beach
in a foaming boil,
Poseidon's treasure.

Conchs roll in shallow froth,
maritime toys in a king's bath;
it is a sea-runic poem from antiquity,
with frosting.

Angry Blue Lady

An angry blue lady
clutches my ankles,
pulls me deeper than I want.

Her tantrum,
a shining bluster,
glints in the sun.

I squint; only yesterday
she gently mimed the
dove grey sky.

Twilight

Sunlight pauses to meet the night,
lips puckered for a kiss,
dusk considering,
approaching
like a timid lover.

Nebulous
sunset folds into darkness;
twilight and surf,
the rising moon
gathers twelve hours into its arms.

No Despair

There is no despair by the sea,
when it is greenly blue,
swells winking
in the noon time sun.

There's no room for tears.
The sea laughs at them,
wipes them with foggy fingers,
makes one whole.
It cajoles gently to hope,

shows its tideline from last night,
whispers, More will come.
It is faithful as the tide is strong;
there is no despair by the sea.

Patina

Windhovered words
were falcon's
flight,
half-prayers
to perse deities
reigning at the horizon.

Tears sought sand,
a bitter, salted patina,
absorbed,
collected out of sight,
whether as precious or shameful
I could not discern.

Heaven's Template

A salty breeze swerves
the crests,
toppling tottering breakers.

The cottage,
clam shells on its roof,
hides behind dunes;

somber slatted fences
jig in the wind,
sea grasses clapping at their feet.

We will bask here in the sun,
touching where none have touched,
as none have touched,

collecting sea spray and pristine sky,
wondering all the while
if this be heaven's template.

Swell

Ocean floor
curves into smooth
valleys beneath
thrusting tipped-toes.

A swell lifts,
gives view
of a fishing trawler
tracing the teal skyline.

Hankering for sand castles,
the wave restores feet to
sand, plunges hungrily
toward the beach once more.

Stained

Greedy for possession,
sun leaves prints
on what it does not own,
casts the world
in its auric mask.

Twilight requisition
spills fire paint
from the horizon,
a path from the sun,
a coral veneer on the sea.

Aburst in breeze,
toes plying sand,
I am marked;
even pain is stained
by solar interference.

Two Crafts

A charter boat drones
a spumy trail
toward the horizon,
prickly antennae and poles astir
like positioned stingers.

Two crafts pass,
the smaller
bouncing in swells;
motors silenced,
fishermen grip hope in their hands.

Almost Young

A grey-haired woman pulls
on a tight blue swim cap,
the kind women used to wear.

Sidestepping sand castles, she gingerly
crosses the beach toward lines of
surf that stretch beyond the jetty.

Froth leaps around her legs; she
steps over low breakers, dives
into a burgeoning bearded wave,

swims with surprising strength
toward deep water,
blue cap marking her progress.

Her years remain onshore; she is
almost young again among the rolling
swells of a timeless sea.

Intervals

Running into the sea,
shells underfoot,
swimmers cleave baby breakers,

plunge into towering spindrifts
crowned with sunlit shards,
fleeced coils sliding toward the beach,

groundswells singing
spumescent intervals
of a perfect whitecapped song.

Scooped

A ruffled toddler painstakingly worked her way
across the beach, conquering
turreted forts and sunken footprints
'til she tottered with success at our feet.

Brushing sandy hands, she raised her
eyes, smile fading into sudden panic;
rescued from mistaken destination, she was
scooped mid-wail into her mother's arms.

Diamonds

Neck deep in diamonds,
grasping sun stippled froth,

hang gliding on a five foot wave
above the face of the sea,
I'm a child soaring
in my father's arms,

neck deep in diamonds,
grasping sun stippled froth.

Moment

The wave approaches;
knees bent,
right foot presses seafloor
to launch a
looping sunward glide.

White-lipped curls demand both feet,
higher than before,
younger than before -
a smiling child for a
rolling crested moment.

Sea Sprayed Altitude

Sea and sun
are tandem complements;
crystal green water
arcs gently toward new heights,
buoyancy for work-wearied
spirits needing
sea sprayed altitude.

Link in the Silver Chain

They sat on the sand at water's edge,
surf surging, consuming,
receding meekly into the sea.

His son leaned against him,
excited child's voice
a flashback to his own boyhood.

Fifty waves later,
they had carried handfuls of shells
to their blanket;

fifty waves later, they had crafted a
memory, had forged a link
in the silver chain of the sea.

Three Gulls

Their webbed feet
shod with sea foam,
three gulls stood near
folding surf,

wanting fish
served fresh with a
wink of the solar waiter's
glinting eye.

The Fisherman

Hip jutted
to one side,
the fisherman

casts beyond the
breakers, surf curling
around his legs

like frothing ancient
lace that disintegrates
in each breath of the sea.

Thunder Songs

Dunes rest near the sea,
where breakers roar
thunder songs all day.

Sea grasses
stretch and yawn
in misted sunlight;

wind patrols the beach,
a flustered scout,
ruffling gull feathers at noon.

Seabreezes

Seabreezes
wiggled an umbrella,
ransacked sunbathers'
hair with mad creativity,

ran along pinnacles
of the waves,
Poseidon's stepping stones.

They tossed spray to douse the sun,
enough and to spare,
carrying residual mist inland to
coat windows there.

Port

A port
near approaching dawn
is a healing place

where tears are stanched,
where wounds are bound
like a sun-swathed face in June,

where sorrows are ashes
borne away in
breakers' teeth.

The Shell Seeker

Plastic bag in hand,
she walks the tideline
for Neptune's baubles,
strewn last night
on the sand.

Baseball cap
taming wind-stressed hair,
head inclined,
she searches for starfish,

sea horse or conch,
a shell seeker,
heir of shell seekers,
prizing the sea's
largesse, greeting
dawn to find it.

First Sight

Grandma stooped to him,
her arm around his shoulders.
She pointed at the waves.
"Do you want to wade in the sea?"

His face struggled
between curiosity and
restraint, a study of
three year old wisdom.

Standing, she led him by
hand toward the harmless
froth that slid shells
around their toes.

Ankle deep, the little boy
began a lurching, kick-splashing dance,
first sight of the sea,
first steps in devotion.

Where Water Thunders

When a salty wind
strides the beach to tap my shoulder,
I feel your touch.

When I lay back, toes wiggling in sand,
eyes closed to the sun's blazing glare,
I see your face.

I find you
where water thunders, where sea
mist walks forever on the wind.

Lunar Direction

A gigantic ad hovers,
a jovial entrepreneur
who deals in oceanfront property.

The sea calls it an honest face,
lunges toward shore
to buy beaches from the moon man.

Tide caters to the moon,
listens for first footfall in the sky,
for whispered lunar direction.

Flash of Silver

The fisherman throws them back;
his desire is battle,
not fillets,

the heavy pulsing
of line's fruition,
the chatter of bowed rod,
the reeling in,
catch breaking through surf
with a flash of silver.

One cast begets
another as the sun sinks with
approval into the bay.

Hesperus by the Bay

Gulls swoop over receding
water to perch on pylons
of a vanished dock.
The shack by the causeway
is no one's desire,
a fragmented dream
gone wrong.

Ruined windows, derelict door,
threadbare roof defy
seasons; no one braves the
ravaged porch.
The bay rejected the
house long ago,
nature's joke.

People passing on the bridge
smirk at this ruin;
they do not know its story,
nor whose it was. Now it belongs
to gulls, to wild marsh things,
and somehow to us all -
a broken Hesperus by the bay.

Atlantic City

Atlantic City's
white capped seniors
make pilgrimages to shrines,
huge temples by the sea.

Trumped and having dined
with Caesar, they patrol
the boardwalk beneath an
autumn sun.

These seniors are
seasoned and comfortable
among phantom,
favored odds.

Buses bring them
to the shore,
where they grace Fate
with white hair and moxie.

Foreign Path

The future's voice is
a foreign path at sunrise,
eloquent with
salmon syntax
in the eastern sky.

Dawn travelers
begin their journey
beneath fading stars,
a footfall toward the sun,
a foothold by the sea.

Barnegat Light

Determined as yesterday's gale,
a red and white
lighthouse propositions
the sea, warns crafts
of phantom sand bars,
of rocky crags
at the cusp of the island.

Last night's full moon
painted the sky silver,
echoed the lighthouse's
prismed voice
at land's edge, light
and ocean waves
mingled a mile at sea.

Acquisition

The beach near the lighthouse
slides into the sea,

sand to sand
onslaught,
one tide anticipating another.

Ocean froths with acquisition,
roars greedy chants at landfall,
determined,

exhausts Neptune's patience,
casts diamonds ashore
in exchange for dunes -

perpetual patron,
spindrift spendthrift.

Seven Days

The island offers a causeway's
welcome, bay sails taut,
ship's anchor grinning beneath the
snapping post office flag;

children with spades
race to a beach
pocked with clam
shells, where sea
grasses graze
salt breezes.
They cover with sand
the tyranny of
three hundred days,

digging ocean-filled holes
where dunes guard first land,
where terns and gulls
hunt tiny crabs for lunch,
where horizon restrains the sea
in sweeping panorama,
claiming sky and surging water
as its own.

Seven days afford
salty release,
connection to a child's
vista of the sea.

Sea at Dusk

Waves unroll,
lunge toward dry sand;
a grey veil
filters the view,
eases the day's hold.

I wish you were here
to grasp my hand,
to gaze with me,
even if all we did is listen
to the song of the sea at dusk.

Salty Queue

We are bestowed with souvenirs
from the last high tide,
a salty queue
of seaweed and shells,
residue of angry sea
and nor'wester,
midnight's August storm.
Our footprints on wet sand
trail us companionably
like a faithful dog
at sunrise.

Launch

Swells humped heart-high
as evening pulled a hat
low on its radiant brow;
meandering, windy fingers
spun fantasy in our hair.
The launch severed
a flourish of whitecaps,
wooden bow hugging
the crystal breast below it.

Your words were stars,
plucked from the night;
at your voice,
gulls ceased their banter.
With each touch
there was one more memory
to be examined later
in the rekindled light
of an uncharted day.

Rain on the Coast

There will be rain enough
to fill gullies,
greyness enough
to blur my sight.

There will be rain tonight,
darkly bleeding crystal,
tides straining
for higher ground,
surf thundering,
slapping beaches with breaker fists.

There will be rain enough
to fill the skies,
storm enough
to disquiet my senses.

Summer Souvenirs

It vanishes like vapor,
like forgotten echoes;
intransient time
will not be bullied.

The days of August are a memory:
August caresses,
August smiles,
August laughter
are my summer souvenirs.

Morning Gift

The morning beach is a knobby
carpet beneath each footstep,
an uneven path graced
with ocean trinkets.

Spindrifts rise,
uncurl with
crash and swirl,
shout secrets to the beach.

Gulls sing,
plunge breakfast-driven
into the sea
beneath the sun's raised fist,

dawn's victory.
Stars are exchanged for daylight;
I receive the gift quietly,
countenance toward the wind.

Time Is Not a Player

A mahogany boat
joins the sea,
each rise and fall a journey.

Here is a mystery place,
swollen with ancient waters,

a mystical craft
where a poet's words
entwine with yearning.

Love is the mystery,
and time is not a player.

Tackle

Fog is nature's breath,
a misty greeting
near water at dawn.
Ripples betray sunlit awakening;
day is reborn where darkness slept.

A boat scrapes the
shoulders of the shore,
eases into lapping whitecaps,
nudges shells on shells,
slides into an expectant sea.

Rods and tackle are heaven's toys;
each cast is a prayer.

Stylus

Bare feet press chilled sand
like a stylus,
footprint font,
writing the first lines of a memory
on the portal of the sea.

Sparking with coral
cadences, the ocean
bellows our names,
beckons bygone days,
deludes time once again at sunset.

Cement Ship

Plundered,
broken,
borne with despair
on the shoulders of the sea,

her keening voice
echoed in tide that
surged through her like
ill-fated krill.

Asleep on jasmine
bluffs, the coral sun
watched breakers
taste her,

saw seals, pelicans,
sea ducks and swooping gulls -
new life in her womb -
establish sanctuary.

The cement ship froths
with promise, renews
the dignity of refuge
with every salt-glazed dawn.

The Sea Wife

The ocean stole him,
charmed her man
with chanteys and tales
of pirates' treasure.

Tears woven with mist,
Eva climbs a dune each day,
censures this
remorseless blue woman.

The water does not care;
she ignores Eva,
sorts azure gems glinting faceted
fire in the late summer sun.

Eva mourns her loss;
the sea wife's salted prayers
and whispered curses
mingle at high tide.

Tracks Upon the Sand

That's the way it goes, they've said,
time's footprints crease our brows;
we all succomb to charmless days
for such our age allows.

But wait, we carry journey's tales
within each fisted hand,
and look, those lines upon our face
are tracks upon the sand.

Mindscapes

Fantasies
glide like gulls
at noon
above the sea's agitation.

Nurtured by their magic,
we soar with imagination's
eager wings,
creating mindscapes at mid-day.

Neighbor

The sea pours
like molten glass
onto the beach,

laps children's toes,
nibbles the beach's nose,
erodes dunes at high tide.

Some choose the ocean
as neighbor; they do
not mind its antics.

The water calls them by name,
lures them with shells, waves
and aqua continuity.

Stunt Man

Poseidon rolls toward shore,
row after row,
shoulders shrugging,
breaker breath bubbling
onto the sand.

It is a movie,
employing one stunt man
to do the same
rolling
trick
all day long.

Wet Sand

The beach near the water
is dimpled with footprints,
strewn with sea sighs
and frothy toys.

Hair frisks about faces,
salted Medusas.

Our ankles sink into
wet sand,
the ocean's shameless
effort to detain us.

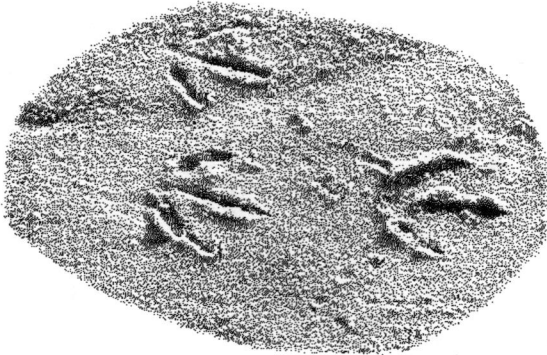

Child's Wonder

Neptune's songs
peel from the water
toward heaped dunes;
listen by the sea
with a child's wonder.

Tidal pools capture
crabs and driftwood,
shells draping seaweed;
pause by the sea
with a child's wonder.

Dawn's coral solitude
is a prayer that
greets each new day;
renew by the sea
with a child's wonder.

Saturday Night

The moon preens on
Saturday night,
changes its shirt,
winks at smiling girls,
nods at surf straining
toward the tide line
on moonlit feet.
It is Saturday night;
the beach has a date
with the moon.

Serenade

The sea is a rolling musician;
its water'd music and lyrics
tangle with the wails
of channel buoys and windblown hair.

Breaker fingers strum the beach
in measured froth,
a serenade for sea-souls
on holiday.

Houseboat

Preening in the sun,
a whitewashed houseboat
rocks in silence, waiting
for the weekenders to arrive.

Music will shred the darkness,
hours will sail passion's current
to a gull-and-channel fugue,
seagirt renewal.

Face of the Sea

Haze cloaks dawn
like a grey woolen wrap;
buoy bells chime
with the piercing cries
of hungry gulls.

Horizon's fireball
rolls slowly toward the heights
of newborn sky,
paints red clouds
above the azure face of the sea.

A Breaker's Aria

The sea warbles chanteys
spun from pirates' songs
and clatter of shells
in the cellar of the sea.

Night hums Andromeda's lullaby
with dissonant bass buoys,
ancient music,
a breaker's aria.

Sojourners

Charting courses for
distant ports,
unknown harbors,
we are sojourners

lured by possibility,
night navigators
surging on the curve
of the sea -

nurturing breast -
one ship
sharing in common
the challenges of destination.

Against the Tide

She aimlessly traces
the waterline at dusk,
explosive surf
straining to lap
serpentine
trailing footprints.

Her red hair,
a dervish in
wet sea breeze,
blazes in frenzy;
she shoves
it from her eyes.

Gulls glide by,
hover over breakers.
She pauses,
watches,
tears and mist undefined,
unable to surge
against the tide.

Blue Visage

The morning fog
is a misty,
lingering caress
on horizon's
pale grey cheek.

Surf is a muse
bidding landlocked
dreams set sail;
the blue visage of the sea
is possibility.

Aura

Children dig
sand castles at
the feet of the tide.

Prone to change,
we seek the
constancy of the sea;

sand is less predictable,
shifting under our toes,
malleable.

In the aura of the sea,
we are all children.

Tears of the Moon

The ocean is restless,
dark eyes glinting
at Orion.

Moon spews refracted light
on sprindrifts,
white-haired dancers
bent on beach performances.

Waves bellow fog songs all
night, while the sea
catches the tears of the moon.

Dawn Strains Closer

The world sleeps,
captured in the breath
of cold darkness;
dawn strains closer.

Night scrambles away,
leaving molten etchings
in its wake, misted firesteps
to scorch sea's blushing face,

to collect goldplated
shells at high tide,
whose mark meanders
on sand near our feet.

Opus in the Sky

Night of plenty, passion swirling,
ancient light upon each crest,
seaborne mist adrift with buoys
softly sings where seagulls nest.

Breakers swell with voices rising,
crash with foam around my feet,
capture glints of star-crazed heaven
where the sky and ocean meet.

Moments of perfection seized from
sole encounter's stolen sigh,
vast unerring midnight treasure,
star-hewn opus in the sky.

Take Home the Sea

Find sea souvenirs,
summer memories for
snowy December nights;
take deep salted breaths
laced with surf applause
and sea spray.

Know one more wave;
vacation ends tomorrow.
Get souvenirs tonight,
more shells,
surf and moonlight -
take home the sea.

Order Form

Take Home the Sea

Send a copy of
Take Home the Sea
to a friend.

It's a great gift idea for the
seashore lover.

Take Home the Sea
Order Form

You can order online at **www.daysofyore.org**
email: books@daysofyore.org
Fax: 810-222-7532
Or send check or money order to:
Days of Yore Publishing
P.O. Box 166,   Fountainville, PA 18923

Your Name: _____

Address: _____

_____

City: _____

State: _____   Zip: _____

Your Email: _____

Credit Card #:_____

Visa ____   M/C ____   Expiration date_____

Signature: _____

Numbers of Copies: _____

Pricing: Take Home the Sea, $13.95 US
            Buy 5 and get the 6th one free.
Shipping by Air:
US: First book, $4.00, each additional book, $ .50
International: First book, $8.00, each additional book, $1.00
Sales Tax: PA residents add 6% sales tax